LIFE *Lessons*

WITH MAX LUCADO

CONTENTS

HOW TO
STUDY THE BIBLE

This is a peculiar book you are holding. Words crafted in another language. Deeds done in a distant era. Events recorded in a far-off land. Counsel offered to a foreign people. This is a peculiar book.

It's surprising that anyone reads it. It's too old. Some of its writings date back five thousand years. It's too bizarre. The book speaks of incredible floods, fires, earthquakes, and people with supernatural abilities. It's too radical. The Bible calls for undying devotion to a carpenter who called himself God's Son.

Logic says this book shouldn't survive. Too old, too bizarre, too radical.

The Bible has been banned, burned, scoffed, and ridiculed. Scholars have mocked it as foolish. Kings have branded it as illegal. A thousand times over, the grave has been dug and the dirge has begun, but somehow the Bible never stays in the grave. Not only has it survived; it has thrived. It is the single most popular book in all of history. It has been the best-selling book in the world for years!

There is no way on earth to explain it. Which perhaps is the only explanation. The answer? The Bible's durability is not found on earth; it is found in heaven. For the millions who have tested its claims and claimed its promises, there is but one answer: the Bible is God's book and God's voice.

As you read it, you would be wise to give some thought to two questions. What is the purpose of the Bible? and How do I study the Bible? Time spent reflecting on these two issues will greatly enhance your Bible study.

What is the purpose of the Bible?

Let the Bible itself answer that question.

Since you were a child you have known the Holy Scriptures which are able to make you wise. And that wisdom leads to salvation through faith in Christ Jesus. (2 Tim. 3:15 NCV)

The purpose of the Bible? Salvation. God's highest passion is to get his children home. His book, the Bible, describes his plan of salvation. The purpose of the Bible is to proclaim God's plan and passion to save his children.

That is the reason this book has endured through the centuries. It dares to tackle the toughest questions about life: Where do I go after I die? Is there a God? What do I do with my fears? The Bible offers answers to these crucial questions. It is the treasure map that leads us to God's highest treasure—eternal life.

LIFE
Lessons

WITH MAX LUCADO

BOOK OF HEBREWS

THE INCOMPARABLE CHRIST

MAX LUCADO

Prepared by

THE LIVINGSTONE CORPORATION

NELSON IMPACT

A Division of Thomas Nelson Publishers

Since 1798

Published by Nelson Impact, a Division of Thomas Nelson, Inc., P.O. Box 141000, Nashville, Tennessee, 37214.

Produced with the assistance of the Livingstone Corporation (www.livingstonecorp.com). Project staff include Jake Barton, Joel Bartlett, Andy Culbertson, and Mary Horner Collins.

Editor: Neil Wilson

Scripture quotations marked "NCV™" are taken from the New Century Version®. Copyright © 2005 by Thomas Nelson, Inc. Used by permission. All rights reserved.

Scripture quotations marked "NKJV™" are taken from the New King James Version®. Copyright © 1982 by Thomas Nelson, Inc. Used by permission. All rights reserved.

Scripture quotations marked (NIV) are taken from the Holy Bible, New International Version. Copyright © 1973, 1978, 1984 by International Bible Society. All rights reserved. Used by permission of Zondervan Publishing House.

Scripture quotations marked (PHILLIPS) are taken from the New Testament in Modern English translated by J. B. Phillips. Copyright © 1958, 1959, 1960, 1972 by J. B. Phillips.

Scripture quotations marked (TEV) are taken from the Good News Bible in Today's English Version, Second Edition. Copyright © 1992 by American Bible Society. Used by permission. All rights reserved.

Material for the "Inspiration" sections taken from the following books:

The Applause of Heaven. Copyright © 1990, 1996, 1999 by Max Lucado. W Publishing Group, a Division of Thomas Nelson, Inc., Nashville, Tennessee.

God Came Near. Copyright © 2004 by Max Lucado. W Publishing Group, a Division of Thomas Nelson, Inc., Nashville, Tennessee.

The Great House of God. Copyright © 1997 by Max Lucado. W Publishing Group, a Division of Thomas Nelson, Inc., Nashville, Tennessee.

He Still Moves Stones. Copyright © 1993 by Max Lucado. W Publishing Group, a Division of Thomas Nelson, Inc., Nashville, Tennessee.

It's Not About Me. Copyright © 2004 by Max Lucado. Integrity Publishers, Brentwood, Tennessee.

Just Like Jesus Devotional. Copyright © 2003 by Max Lucado. W Publishing Group, a Division of Thomas Nelson, Inc., Nashville, Tennessee.

Next Door Savior. Copyright © 2003 by Max Lucado. W Publishing Group, a Division of Thomas Nelson, Inc., Nashville, Tennessee.

Shaped by God (previously published as *On the Anvil*). Copyright © 2001 by Max Lucado. Tyndale House Publishers, Wheaton, Illinois.

Six Hours One Friday. Copyright © 2004 by Max Lucado. W Publishing Group, a Division of Thomas Nelson, Inc., Nashville, Tennessee.

Walking with Christ in the Details of Life. Copyright © 1992 by Patrick Morley. Thomas Nelson, Inc., Nashville, Tennessee.

Cover Art and Interior Design by Kirk Luttrell of the Livingstone Corporation

Interior Composition by Rachel Hawkins of the Livingstone Corporation

ISBN-13: 978-1-4185-0955-2

But how do we use the Bible? Countless copies of Scripture sit unread on book-shelves and nightstands simply because people don't know how to read it. What can we do to make the Bible real in our lives?

The clearest answer is found in the words of Jesus. He promised:

Ask, and God will give to you. Search, and you will find. Knock, and the door will open for you. (Matt. 7:7 NCV)

The first step in understanding the Bible is asking God to help us. We should read prayerfully. If anyone understands God's Word, it is because of God and not the reader.

But the Helper will teach you everything and will cause you to remember all that I told you. The Helper is the Holy Spirit whom the Father will send in my name. (John 14:26 NCV)

Before reading the Bible, pray. Invite God to speak to you. Don't go to Scripture looking for your idea; go searching for his.

Not only should we read the Bible prayerfully; we should read it carefully. *Search and you will find* is the pledge. The Bible is not a newspaper to be skimmed but rather a mine to be quarried.

Search for it like silver, and hunt for it like hidden treasure. Then you will understand respect for the Lord, and you will find that you know God. (Prov. 2:4–5 NCV)

Any worthy find requires effort. The Bible is no exception. To understand the Bible you don't have to be brilliant, but you must be willing to roll up your sleeves and search.

Be a worker who is not ashamed and who uses the true teaching in the right way. (2 Tim. 2:15 NCV)

Here's a practical point. Study the Bible a bit at a time. Hunger is not satisfied by eating twenty-one meals in one sitting once a week. The body needs a steady diet to remain strong. So does the soul. When God sent food to his people in the wilderness, he didn't provide loaves already made. Instead, he sent them manna in the shape of *"thin flakes like frost . . . on the desert ground"* (Ex. 16:14 NCV).

God gave manna in limited portions. God sends spiritual food the same way. He opens the heavens with just enough nutrients for today's hunger. He provides *"a command here, a command there. A rule here, a rule there. A little lesson here, a little lesson there"* (Isa. 28:10 NCV).

Don't be discouraged if your reading reaps a small harvest. Some days a lesser portion is all that is needed. What is important is to search every day for that day's message. A steady diet of God's Word over a lifetime builds a healthy soul and mind.

A little girl returned from her first day at school. Her mom asked, "Did you learn anything?"

"Apparently not enough," the girl responded, "I have to go back tomorrow and the next day and the next . . ."

Such is the case with learning. And such is the case with Bible study. Understanding comes little by little over a lifetime.

There is a third step in understanding the Bible. After the asking and seeking comes the knocking. After you ask and search, then knock.

Knock, and the door will open for you. (Matt. 7:7 NCV)

To knock is to stand at God's door. To make yourself available. To climb the steps, cross the porch, stand at the doorway, and volunteer. Knocking goes beyond the realm of thinking and into the realm of acting.

To knock is to ask, What can I do? How can I obey? Where can I go?

It's one thing to know what to do. It's another to do it. But for those who do it, those who choose to obey, a special reward awaits them.

The truly happy are those who carefully study God's perfect law that makes people free, and they continue to study it. They do not forget what they heard, but they obey what God's teaching says. Those who do this will be made happy. (James 1:25 NCV)

What a promise. Happiness comes to those who do what they read! It's the same with medicine. If you only read the label but ignore the pills, it won't help. It's the same with food. If you only read the recipe but never cook, you won't be fed. And it's the same with the Bible. If you only read the words but never obey, you'll never know the joy God has promised.

Ask. Search. Knock. Simple, isn't it? Why don't you give it a try? If you do, you'll see why you are holding the most remarkable book in history.

INTRODUCTION TO
THE BOOK OF HEBREWS

The best just got better—it's a favorite slogan with advertisers.

It's not that our previous product was poor. It's just that the current one is superior.

The book of Hebrews might well use the same slogan. The best just got better.

There was nothing inferior about the Jewish religion. It was given by God and designed by God. Every principle, rule, and ritual had a wealth of meaning. The Old Testament served as a faithful guide for thousands of people over thousands of years. It was the best offered to man.

But when Christ came, the best got better.

Hebrews was written for Jewish believers who were torn between their new faith and their old ways. The temptation was to slip back into familiar routines and rituals, settling for second best.

The author skillfully makes a case against such a digression. He argues that Jesus is better than every form of the old faith—better than the angels (1:4–2:18), better than the believers' leaders (3:1–4:13), and better than their priests (4:14–7:28). When it comes to comparing the two, there is simply no comparison. Christianity has a better covenant (8:1–13), a better sanctuary, (9:1–10), and a better sacrifice for sins (9:11–10:18).

It's not that the old law was bad; it's just that the new law—salvation by faith in Christ—is better. Once you've known the best, why settle for second rate?

It's doubtful that you will ever be tempted to exchange your faith for an ancient system of priests and sacrifices. But you will be tempted to exchange it for something inferior. If you are reading Hebrews, be reminded: Once you've known the best, why settle for anything less? (Hmmm, there's another catchy slogan.)

LESSON ONE

JESUS
UNDERSTANDS US

MAX
LUCADO

REFLECTION

Think for a moment about how you cope with hurts and disappointments. These are the bumps and bruises we gather almost every day. Some last a brief time; others stay with us for life. Where do you usually turn for comfort when you are hurting?

SITUATION

The writer of Hebrews intended to highlight the uniqueness of Christ. From the first sentence of this letter to the last, Jesus is presented as the final word from God. In that day, there was a fascination with angels among the Jewish culture, but the author made it clear that angels pale in comparison to God's Son. The point was not to disparage angels but to demonstrate the surpassing greatness of Christ and his effective ministry on behalf of those he came to save.

OBSERVATION

Read Hebrews 2:10–18 from the NCV or the NKJV.

NCV

¹⁰God is the One who made all things, and all things are for his glory. He wanted to have many children share his glory, so he made the One who leads people to salvation perfect through suffering.

¹¹Jesus, who makes people holy, and those who are made holy are from the same family. So he is not ashamed to call them his brothers and sisters. ¹²He says,

"Then, I will tell my fellow Israelites about you;

I will praise you in the public meeting."

¹³He also says,

"I will trust in God."

And he also says,

"I am here, and with me are the children God has given me."

¹⁴Since these children are people with physical bodies, Jesus himself became like them. He did this so that, by dying, he could destroy the one who has the power of death—the devil—¹⁵and free those who were like slaves all their lives because of their fear of death. ¹⁶Clearly, it is not angels that Jesus helps, but the people who are from Abraham. ¹⁷For this reason Jesus had to be made like his brothers in every way so he could be their merciful and faithful high priest in service to God. Then Jesus could bring forgiveness for their sins. ¹⁸And now he can help those who are tempted, because he himself suffered and was tempted.

NKJV

¹⁰For it was fitting for Him, for whom are all things and by whom are all things, in bringing many sons to glory, to make the captain of their salvation perfect through sufferings. ¹¹For both He who sanctifies and those who are being sanctified are all of one, for which reason He is not ashamed to call them brethren, ¹²saying:

"I will declare Your name to My brethren;

In the midst of the assembly I will sing praise to You."

¹³And again:

"I will put My trust in Him."

And again:

"Here am I and the children whom God has given Me."

¹⁴Inasmuch then as the children have partaken of flesh and blood, He Himself likewise shared in the same, that through death He might destroy him who had the power of death, that is, the devil, ¹⁵and release those who through fear of death were all their lifetime subject to bondage. ¹⁶For indeed He does not give aid to angels, but He does give aid to the seed of Abraham. ¹⁷Therefore, in all things He had to be made like His brethren, that He might be a merciful and faithful High Priest in things pertaining to God, to make propitiation for the sins of the people. ¹⁸For in that He Himself has suffered, being tempted, He is able to aid those who are tempted.

EXPLORATION

1. Why did God allow his Son to suffer?

2. What effect did Jesus' victory over death have on Satan?

3. What can free people from their fear of death?

4. Why is Jesus the perfect High Priest for us?

5. In what ways is Jesus able to help us?

INSPIRATION

Abandon. Such a haunting word.

On the edge of the small town sits a decrepit house. Weeds higher than the porch. Boarded windows and a screen door bouncing in the wind. To the front gate is nailed a sign: *Abandoned.* No one wants the place. Even the poor and desperate pass it by.

A social worker appears at the door of an orphanage. In her big hand is the small dirty one of a six-year-old girl. As the adults speak, the wide eyes of the child explore the office of the director. She hears the worker whisper, "Abandoned. She was abandoned."

An elderly woman in a convalescent home rocks alone in her room on Christmas. No cards, no calls, no carols.

A young wife discovers romantic e-mails sent by her husband to another woman.

After thirty years on the factory line, a worker finds a termination notice taped to his locker.

Abandoned by family.

Abandoned by a spouse.

Abandoned by big business.

But nothing compares to being abandoned by God.

"At noon the whole country was covered with darkness, which lasted for three hours. At about three o'clock Jesus cried out with a loud shout, 'Eli, Eli, lema sabachthani?' which means, 'My God, my God, why did you abandon me?'" (Matt. 27:45–46 TEV).

By the time Christ screams these words, he has hung on the cross for six hours. Around nine o'clock in the morning, he stumbled to the cleft of Skull Hill. A soldier pressed a knee on his forearm and drove a spike through one hand, then the other, then both feet. As the Romans lifted the cross, they unwittingly placed Christ in the very position in which he came to die—between man and God.

A priest on his own altar. (From *Next Door Savior* by Max Lucado)

REACTION

6. How are Jesus' pain and temptation relevant to us?

7. In times of trouble, why do we turn to other people rather than to Jesus?

8. In what way does God equip us to reach out to others with compassion?

9. How should Christians respond to the pain that comes their way?

10. How has knowing Jesus increased your sensitivity to and compassion for others?

11. What can you do to show God's love to someone who is hurting?

LIFE LESSONS

One of the times we tend to feel alone is when we are facing temptation. It's common for us to think our struggle is unique. But this passage reminds us that Jesus knows what we face. He "gets" it. He has faced the same temptations. He knows. He understands. He wants to help. Will we let him?

DEVOTION

Lord, we stand in awe of you for what you have done—you left your throne to live among us; you faced temptation, ridicule, and shame so that you could understand us; and then you died on a cross to save us from our sins. You gave up everything so that we could spend eternity with you. Help us to grasp the depth of your love. And as we experience your great love for us, help us to share it with others.

For more Bible passages about Jesus' ability to help hurting people, see Job 36:15; Psalms 46:1; 121:1–2; 147:1–5; Isaiah 41:10; 53:3–5; Romans 8:26–27.

To complete the book of Hebrews during this twelve-part study, read Hebrews 1:1–2:18.

JOURNALING

How has Jesus shown his love for me? How can I thank him?

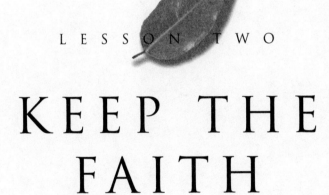

LESSON TWO

KEEP THE
FAITH

MAX
LUCADO

REFLECTION

Recall a time when a Christian friend encouraged your faith. Describe your situation at the time and what specific actions or statements that person used to help you. What have been the long-term results of that person's ministry?

SITUATION

In the hierarchy of Jewish heroes, none equaled Moses, the giver of God's Law and leader of the great exodus from Egypt. He exhibited every aspect of strong spiritual and moral leadership. In the history of Israel no one seemed to have done more than Moses. And yet, the writer of Hebrews says that he was nothing compared to Jesus, God's Son. As he was faithful, we, too, should keep the faith to the end.

OBSERVATION

Read Hebrews 3:1–14 from the NCV or the NKJV.

NCV

¹So all of you holy brothers and sisters, who were called by God, think about Jesus, who was sent to us and is the high priest of our faith. ²Jesus was faithful to God as Moses was in God's family. ³Jesus has more honor than Moses, just as the builder of a house has more honor than the house itself. ⁴Every house is built by someone, but the builder of everything is God himself. ⁵Moses was faithful in God's family as a servant, and he told what God would say in the future. ⁶But Christ is faithful as a Son over God's house. And we are God's house if we keep on being very sure about our great hope.

⁷So it is as the Holy Spirit says:

"Today listen to what he says.

⁸Do not be stubborn as in the past

when you turned against God,

when you tested God in the desert.

⁹There your ancestors tried me and tested me

and saw the things I did for forty years.

¹⁰I was angry with them.

I said, 'They are not loyal to me

and have not understood my ways.'

¹¹I was angry and made a promise,

'They will never enter my rest.' "

¹²So brothers and sisters, be careful that none of you has an evil, unbelieving heart that will turn you away from the living God. ¹³But encourage each other every day while it is "today." Help each other so none of you will become hardened because sin has tricked you. ¹⁴We all share in Christ if we keep till the end the sure faith we had in the beginning.

NKJV

¹Therefore, holy brethren, partakers of the heavenly calling, consider the Apostle and High Priest of our confession, Christ Jesus, ²who was faithful to Him who appointed Him, as Moses also was faithful in all His house. ³For this One has been counted worthy of more glory than Moses, inasmuch as He who built the house has more honor than the house. ⁴For every house is built by someone, but He who built all things is God. ⁵And Moses indeed was faithful in all His house as a servant, for a testimony of those things which would be spoken afterward, ⁶but Christ as a Son over His own house, whose house we are if we hold fast the confidence and the rejoicing of the hope firm to the end.

"Today, if you will hear His voice,

[8]Do not harden your hearts as in the rebellion,

In the day of trial in the wilderness,

[9]Where your fathers tested Me, tried Me,

And saw My works forty years.

[10]Therefore I was angry with that generation,

And said, 'They always go astray in their heart,

And they have not known My ways.'

[11]So I swore in My wrath,

'They shall not enter My rest.'"

[12]Beware, brethren, lest there be in any of you an evil heart of unbelief in departing from the living God; [13]but exhort one another daily, while it is called "Today," lest any of you be hardened through the deceitfulness of sin. [14]For we have become partakers of Christ if we hold the beginning of our confidence steadfast to the end.

EXPLORATION

1. Why is Jesus worthy of greater honor than Moses? How does the comparison affect Moses?

2. How can people demonstrate that they belong in God's house?

3. What warning does the Holy Spirit give to us?

4. Why do some people turn away from God?

5. What practical advice does this passage offer us on remaining faithful to God?

INSPIRATION

Equipped with the right tools, we can learn to listen to God. What are those tools? Here are the ones I have found helpful.

A regular time and place. Select a slot on your schedule and a corner of your world, and claim it for God. For some it may be best to do this in the morning. "In the morning my prayer comes before you" (Ps. 88:13 NIV). Others prefer the evening and agree with David's prayer: "Let my . . . praise [be] like the evening sacrifice" (Ps. 141:2 NCV). Others prefer many encounters during the day. Apparently the author of Psalm 55 did. He wrote, "Evening, morning and noon I cry out" (v. 17 NIV). Some sit under a tree, others in the kitchen. Maybe your commute to work or your lunch break would be appropriate. Find a time and place that seems right for you.

How much time should you take? As much as you need. Value quality over length. Your time with God should last long enough for you to say what you want and for God to say what he wants.

Which leads us to a second tool you need—*an open Bible.* God speaks to us through his Word. The first step in reading the Bible is to ask God to help you understand it. "But the Helper will teach you everything and will cause you to remember all that I told you. This Helper is the Holy Spirit whom the Father will send in my name" (John 14:26 NCV) . . . Will I learn what God intends? If I listen, I will.

There is a third tool for having a productive time with God. Not only do we need a regular time and an open Bible, *we also need a listening heart.* Don't forget the admonition from James: "The man who looks into the perfect mirror of God's law, the law of liberty, and makes a habit of so doing, is not the man who sees and forgets. He puts the law into practice and he wins true happiness" (James 1:25 PHILLIPS).

We know we are listening to God when what we read in the Bible is what others see in our lives. It's one thing not to know. It's another to know and not learn. Paul urged his readers, "Whatever you have learned and received and heard from me, or seen in me, put it into practice" (Phil. 4:9 NIV).

If you want to be just like Jesus, let God have you. Spend time listening for him until you receive your lesson for the day—then apply it. (From *Just Like Jesus Devotional* by Max Lucado)

REACTION

6. Why should believers distinguish between faith and feelings?

7. How can you determine if your faith is real?

8. What can you do to ensure that your faith will endure?

9. How can you avoid hardening your heart against God?

10. What is the danger for Christians who neglect the fellowship of other believers?

11. What Christian friend can you encourage in spiritual matters? How?

LIFE LESSONS

Both Moses and Christ serve as examples of faithfulness to God. Do we really want to hear God say to us, "Well done, good and faithful servant?" The alternative attitude to God's Word is described as "hardening our heart." We know what this means even when we hear the expression for the first time. We've stiffened our wills, backs, and hearts against others, against God. This is familiar territory for most of us. Is it where we want to live? In contrast, God offers us rest—his rest. (More on this in the next lesson.) Beyond the help God offers, we have one another. This passage reminds us that we ought to have the habit of encouraging others. We can help each other toward faithfulness.

DEVOTION

Father, we ask you to deepen our faith in you. Give us the strength to withstand temptation, overcome doubt, and remain loyal to you. At the end of our lives, may we hear your words, "Well done, my good and faithful servant."

For more Bible passages about remaining faithful, see Deuteronomy 11:13–18; 1 Samuel 12:24; 2 Samuel 22:26; 1 Kings 2:3–4; 2 Chronicles 19:9; Psalm 97:10; Proverbs 28:20; Matthew 25:19–23; 1 Corinthians 4:2; 10:12–13; 3 John 1:3–5; Revelation 2:10; 17:14.

To complete the book of Hebrews during this twelve-part study, read Hebrews 3:1–19.

JOURNALING

What steps can I take this week to strengthen my faith in God?

LESSON THREE

GOD'S REST

MAX LUCADO

REFLECTION

Many people have misconceptions about what it means to find true peace. Reflect on what life is like when peace reigns. When peace is lacking, what's in its place? How would you summarize your personal understanding of peace?

SITUATION

While discussing Israel's experience in the wilderness, the book of Hebrews makes it clear that God intended for his children to enter the Promised Land, a land of rest, peace, and plenty. Due to their disobedience and stubbornness, though, one generation was not allowed to enter that promised rest. Drawing on that historical event that all his Jewish readers would have recognized, the author uses it as a powerful analogy for the deeper and broader "salvation rest" that God calls all believers to enter.

OBSERVATION

Read Hebrews 4:1–11 from the NCV or the NKJV.

NCV

¹Now, since God has left us the promise that we may enter his rest, let us be very careful so none of you will fail to enter. ²The Good News was preached to us just as it was to them. But the teaching they heard did not help them, because they heard it but did not accept it with faith. ³We who have believed are able to enter and have God's rest. As God has said,

> *"I was angry and made a promise, 'They will never enter my rest.'"*

But God's work was finished from the time he made the world. ⁴In the Scriptures he talked about the seventh day of the week: "And on the seventh day God rested from all his works." ⁵And again in the Scripture God said, "They will never enter my rest."

⁶It is still true that some people will enter God's rest, but those who first heard the way to be saved did not enter, because they did not obey. ⁷So God planned another day, called "today." He spoke about that day through David a long time later in the same Scripture used before:

> *"Today listen to what he says. Do not be stubborn."*

⁸We know that Joshua did not lead the people into that rest, because God spoke later about another day. ⁹This shows that the rest for God's people is still coming. ¹⁰Anyone who enters God's rest will rest from his work as God did. ¹¹Let us try as hard as we can to enter God's rest so that no one will fail by following the example of those who refused to obey.

NKJV

¹Therefore, since a promise remains of entering His rest, let us fear lest any of you seem to have come short of it. ²For indeed the gospel was preached to us as well as to them; but the word which they heard did not profit them, not being mixed with faith in those who heard it. ³For we who have believed do enter that rest, as He has said:

> *"So I swore in My wrath, 'They shall not enter My rest,'"*

although the works were finished from the foundation of the world. ⁴For He has spoken in a certain place of the seventh day in this way: "And God rested on the seventh day from all His works"; ⁵and again in this place: "They shall not enter My rest."

⁶Since therefore it remains that some must enter it, and those to whom it was first preached did not enter because of disobedience, ⁷again He designates a certain day, saying in David, "Today," after such a long time, as it has been said:

> *"Today, if you will hear His voice, do not harden your hearts."*

⁸For if Joshua had given them rest, then He would not afterward have spoken of another day. ⁹There remains therefore a rest for the people of God. ¹⁰For he who has entered His rest has himself also ceased from his works as God did from His.

¹¹Let us therefore be diligent to enter that rest, lest anyone fall according to the same example of disobedience.

EXPLORATION

1. What is God's rest?

2. Why won't some people be helped by the gospel?

3. How is God's rest broader than only entering the Promised Land, and how can people today enter God's rest?

4. How can we know that God's rest is still to come in the future?

5. What part of the Hebrew people's experience should Christians avoid following?

INSPIRATION

Sleep is determined to bring the day to a close and joy is determined to stretch the day out as long as possible. One last enchanted kingdom. One last giggle. One last game.

Maybe you are like that. Maybe, if you had your way, your day would never end. Every moment demands to be savored. You resist sleep as long as possible because you love being awake so much. If you are like that, congratulations. If not, welcome to the majority.

Most of us have learned another way of going to bed, haven't we? It's called crash and burn. Life is so full of games that the last thing we want is another one as we are trying to sleep. So, for most of us, it's good-bye world, hello pillow. Sleep, for many, is not a robber but a refuge; eight hours of relief for our wounded souls.

And if you are kept awake, it's not by counting your fingers, but by counting your debts, tasks, or even your tears.

You are tired.

You are weary.

Weary of being slapped by the waves of broken dreams.

Weary of being stepped on and run over in the endless marathon to the top.

Weary of trusting in someone only to have that trust returned in an envelope with no return address.

Weary of staring into the future and seeing only futility.

What steals our childhood zeal? . . . It is this weariness that makes the words of the carpenter so compelling. Listen to them. "Come to me, all you who are weary and burdened and I will give you rest."

Come to me . . . The invitation is to come to him. Why him? He offers the invitation as a penniless rabbi in an oppressed nation. He has no connections with the authorities in Rome. He hasn't written a best-seller or earned a diploma.

Yet, he dares to look into the leathery faces of farmers and tired faces of housewives and offer rest. He looks into the disillusioned eyes of a bartender and makes this paradoxical promise: "Take my yoke upon you and learn from me, for I am gentle and humble in heart, and you will find rest for your souls."

The people came. They came out of the cul-de-sacs and office complexes of their existence and he gave them, not religion, not doctrine, not systems, but rest.

As a result, they called him Lord.

As a result, they called him Savior.

Not so much because of what he said, but because of what he did.

What he did on the cross during six hours, one Friday. (From *Six Hours One Friday* by Max Lucado)

REACTION

6. How does God's rest relate to peace?

7. How can we experience God's rest both now and in the future?

8. What keeps us from enjoying the rest God offers?

9. How is your life different since you first discovered peace with God?

10. In what area of your life are you still not enjoying God's rest?

11. How would you explain God's rest to a non-Christian?

LIFE LESSONS

One of Jesus' specific promises to us has to do with peace. "Peace I leave with you, My peace I give to you; not as the world gives do I give to you. Let not your heart be troubled, neither let it be afraid" (John 14:27 NKJV). Though the world talks about "peace," we know that the peace we have in Christ is something else. God's peace is the rest that comes when we know our lives and our future are in the hands of Someone far more capable than us. The world thinks peace is a state we create by our efforts; Christ offers us peace and asks us to let absolutely nothing keep us from entering it. It's his peace that we get to enjoy.

DEVOTION

We thank you, Father, that we can experience your rest both now and for all of eternity. Teach us to appreciate and enjoy the peace you offer us today. Protect us from unbelief and disobedience so that nothing will keep us from entering your eternal rest.

For more Bible passages about God's rest, see Exodus 31:15–17; 33:14; Psalms 16:9–11; 62:1–5; 95:10–11; 116:7; Isaiah 11:10; Jeremiah 6:16; Matthew 11:28–30; Revelation 14:13.

To complete the book of Hebrews during this twelve-part study, read Hebrews 4:1–13.

JOURNALING

What steps can I take to more fully enjoy God's rest this week?

LESSON FOUR

JESUS,
OUR HIGH
PRIEST

MAX
LUCADO

REFLECTION

Some people think they can't possibly approach God on their own. The book of Hebrews shows that we can approach God's throne directly, even boldly, through Jesus Christ. Think about your religious upbringing. What part did priests or elders or pastors play in your church? When did you realize that, through Christ, you could have a relationship with God directly?

SITUATION

The first four chapters of Hebrews are a *tour de force* of applying the lessons of the Old Testament to contemporary lives. The Jewish readers would have understood these references and the important role of the ancient priests. The high priest was the only one who could enter the Most Holy Place. Once a year, he entered to make the atoning sacrifice for the people's sin. Because of God's holiness, without the priest, no one could approach God. Without the priest, no sacrifice for sin could be offered. After highlighting the powerful and unique role that God's living Word fulfills in the lives of believers (4:12–13), the author describes Jesus' special role as the ultimate High Priest.

OBSERVATION

Read Hebrews 4:14–16 and 5:1–10 from the NCV or the NKJV.

NCV

*4:14*Since we have a great high priest, Jesus the Son of God, who has gone into heaven, let us hold on to the faith we have. *15*For our high priest is able to understand our weaknesses. When he lived on earth, he was tempted in every way that we are, but he did not sin. *16*Let us, then, feel very sure that we can come before God's throne where there is grace. There we can receive mercy and grace to help us when we need it.

*5:1*Every high priest is chosen from among other people. He is given the work of going before God for them to offer gifts and sacrifices for sins. *2*Since he himself is weak, he is able to be gentle with those who do not understand and who are doing wrong things. *3*Because he is weak, the high priest must offer sacrifices for his own sins and also for the sins of the people.

*4*To be a high priest is an honor, but no one chooses himself for this work. He must be called by God as Aaron was. *5*So also Christ did not choose himself to have the honor of being a high priest, but God chose him. God said to him,

> "You are my Son.
>
> Today I have become your Father."

*6*And in another Scripture God says,

> "You are a priest forever,
>
> a priest like Melchizedek."

*7*While Jesus lived on earth, he prayed to God and asked God for help. He prayed with loud cries and tears to the One who could save him from death, and his prayer was heard because he trusted God. *8*Even though Jesus was the Son of God, he learned obedience by what he suffered. *9*And because his obedience was perfect, he was able to give eternal salvation to all who obey him. *10*In this way God made Jesus a high priest, a priest like Melchizedek.

NKJV

*4:14*Seeing then that we have a great High Priest who has passed through the heavens, Jesus the Son of God, let us hold fast our confession. *15*For we do not have a High Priest who cannot sympathize with our weaknesses, but was in all points tempted as we are, yet without sin. *16*Let us therefore come boldly to the throne of grace, that we may obtain mercy and find grace to help in time of need.

*5:1*For every high priest taken from among men is appointed for men in things pertaining to God, that he may offer both gifts and sacrifices for sins. *2*He can have compassion on those who are ignorant and going astray, since he himself is also subject to weakness. *3*Because of this he is required as for the people, so also for himself, to offer sacrifices for sins. *⁴And no man takes this honor to himself, but he who is called by God, just as Aaron was.*

⁵So also Christ did not glorify Himself to become High Priest, but it was He who said to Him:

> *"You are My Son,*
>
> *Today I have begotten You."*

⁶As He also says in another place:

> *"You are a priest forever*
>
> *According to the order of Melchizedek";*

⁷who, in the days of His flesh, when He had offered up prayers and supplications, with vehement cries and tears to Him who was able to save Him from death, and was heard because of His godly fear, ⁸though He was a Son, yet He learned obedience by the things which He suffered. ⁹And having been perfected, He became the author of eternal salvation to all who obey Him, ¹⁰called by God as High Priest "according to the order of Melchizedek."

EXPLORATION

1. With what attitude should Christians approach God's throne? Why?

2. Describe the role and responsibilities of a high priest.

3. What qualified Jesus to become the ultimate High Priest?

4. In what ways was Jesus similar to Melchizedek and other high priests (see Genesis 14:18–20)? How was he different?

5. Why can Jesus offer you eternal salvation?

INSPIRATION

When it comes to the major-league difficulties like death, disease, sin, and disaster—you know that God cares.

But what about the smaller things? What about grouchy bosses or flat tires or lost dogs? What about broken dishes, late flights, toothaches, or a crashed hard disk? Do these matter to God?

I mean, he's got a universe to run. He's got the planets to keep balanced and presidents and kings to watch over. He's got wars to worry with and famines to fix. Who am I to tell him about my ingrown toenail?

I'm glad you asked. Let me tell you who you are. In fact, let me *proclaim* who you are.

You are an heir of God and a co-heir with Christ.

You are eternal, like an angel.

You have a crown that will last forever.

You are a holy priest, a treasured possession.

You were chosen before the creation of the world. You are destined for "praise, fame, and honor, and you will be a holy people to the Lord your God."

But more than any of the above—more significant than any title or position—is the simple fact that you are God's child. "The Father has loved us so much that we are called children of God. And we really are his children" (1 John 3:1 NCV).

I love that last phrase! "We really are his children." It's as if John knew some of us would shake our heads and say, "Naw, not me. Mother Teresa, maybe. Billy Graham, all right. But not me." If those are your feelings, John added that phrase for you.

"We *really* are his children."

As a result, if something is important to you, it's important to God . . . So go ahead. Tell God what hurts. Talk to him. He won't turn you away. He won't think it's silly. "For our high priest is *able to understand* our weaknesses. When he lived on earth, he was tempted in every way that we are, but he did not sin. Let us, then, feel very sure that we can come before God's throne where there is grace" (Heb. 4:15–16 NCV).

Does God care about the little things in our lives? You better believe it. If it matters to you, it matters to him. (From *He Still Moves Stones* by Max Lucado)

REACTION

6. What kind of relationship does Jesus want to have with us?

7. When have you felt reluctant to go to Jesus with a need or concern? Why?

8. Is it possible to carry your burdens alone? How does it feel to release them to God?

9. Why is it important to understand Jesus' role as High Priest?

10. How would your life be different if you released all of your problems to Jesus?

11. What can you do to develop the habit of turning to God with your joys and concerns?

LIFE LESSONS

The title *priest* may convey different meanings to us as one who is a mediator and a representative for us before God. But when such a title is applied to Jesus, it immediately carries more weight. Jesus alone has the unique role of being both High Priest and the ultimate sacrifice. This term reminds us of something we cannot do for ourselves: we cannot meet our own spiritual needs. Second, it reminds us of the cost involved in meeting our spiritual needs: Jesus gave his life for our sin. Third, it calls from us deep respect and obedience. The effectiveness of Jesus' work as our "High Priest" is due to the fact that he experienced real life among us and knows what we go through. In every way, Jesus is worthy of our trust with anything and everything.

DEVOTION

Father, you know our goals and dreams for the future, our deepest hurts and disappointments, even our weaknesses and failures. You understand us completely. Teach us to be open and honest with you, not for your benefit, but for ours.

For more Bible passages about Jesus' relationship with believers, see John 15:5; Romans 5:11; 1 Timothy 1:15; Hebrews 2:9–11; 6:19–20; 7:22–26; 8:1–2; 1 Peter 2:4–10.

To complete the book of Hebrews during this twelve-part study, read Hebrews 4:14–5:14.

JOURNALING

What area of my life have I held back from Jesus? How can I trust him with that part of my life?

PERSEVERANCE

MAX
LUCADO

REFLECTION

The process of having a vision, creating a plan, setting goals, and pursuing them to completion provides deep satisfaction. One of the integral aspects of the process is the willingness to persevere to the end. Think of a time when you worked hard to reach a personal goal. What helped you persevere? How does that apply to your spiritual growth?

SITUATION

Knowing that Jesus is our great High Priest, the author challenged the readers to go on to solid spiritual food. He held up the mirror of Christian maturity before his audience and told them to look and examine themselves. He warned the Hebrew Christians to be diligent and deliberate about going "on to perfection," or spiritual maturity (6:1). We, too, must be diligent and deliberate; we cannot be passive. We must actively receive all that Christ has done for us, make living for him our goal, and persevere to the end.

OBSERVATION

Read Hebrews 6:7–20 from the NCV or the NKJV.

NCV

⁷Some people are like land that gets plenty of rain. The land produces a good crop for those who work it, and it receives God's blessings. ⁸Other people are like land that grows thorns and weeds and is worthless. It is in danger of being cursed by God and will be destroyed by fire.

⁹Dear friends, we are saying this to you, but we really expect better things from you that will lead to your salvation. ¹⁰God is fair; he will not forget the work you did and the love you showed for him by helping his people. And he will remember that you are still helping them. ¹¹We want each of you to go on with the same hard work all your lives so you will surely get what you hope for. ¹²We do not want you to become lazy. Be like those who through faith and patience will receive what God has promised.

¹³God made a promise to Abraham. And as there is no one greater than God, he used himself when he swore to Abraham, ¹⁴saying, "I will surely bless you and give you many descendants." ¹⁵Abraham waited patiently for this to happen, and he received what God promised.

¹⁶People always use the name of someone greater than themselves when they swear. The oath proves that what they say is true, and this ends all arguing. ¹⁷God wanted to prove that his promise was true to those who would get what he promised. And he wanted them to understand clearly that his purposes never change, so he made an oath. ¹⁸These two things cannot change: God cannot lie when he makes a promise, and he cannot lie when he makes an oath. These things encourage us who came to God for safety. They give us strength to hold on to the hope we have been given. ¹⁹We have this hope as an anchor for the soul, sure and strong. It enters behind the curtain in the Most Holy Place in heaven, ²⁰where Jesus has gone ahead of us and for us. He has become the high priest forever, a priest like Melchizedek.

NKJV

⁷For the earth which drinks in the rain that often comes upon it, and bears herbs useful for those by whom it is cultivated, receives blessing from God; ⁸but if it bears thorns and briars, it is rejected and near to being cursed, whose end is to be burned.

⁹But, beloved, we are confident of better things concerning you, yes, things that accompany salvation, though we speak in this manner. ¹⁰For God is not unjust to forget your work and labor of love which you have shown toward His name, in that you have ministered to the saints, and do minister. ¹¹And we desire that each one of you show the same diligence to the full assurance of hope until the end, ¹²that you do not become sluggish, but imitate those who through faith and patience inherit the promises.

¹³*For when God made a promise to Abraham, because He could swear by no one greater, He swore by Himself, ¹⁴saying, "Surely blessing I will bless you, and multiplying I will multiply you." ¹⁵And so, after he had patiently endured, he obtained the promise. ¹⁶For men indeed swear by the greater, and an oath for confirmation is for them an end of all dispute. ¹⁷Thus God, determining to show more abundantly to the heirs of promise the immutability of His counsel, confirmed it by an oath, ¹⁸that by two immutable things, in which it is impossible for God to lie, we might have strong consolation, who have fled for refuge to lay hold of the hope set before us.*

¹⁹*This hope we have as an anchor of the soul, both sure and steadfast, and which enters the Presence behind the veil, ²⁰where the forerunner has entered for us, even Jesus, having become High Priest forever according to the order of Melchizedek.*

EXPLORATION

1. Whom does God bless? Whom does he curse? What results from God's blessings and curses?

2. How does God demonstrate his fairness to his people?

3. What promise has God given us? How do we know that the promise is secure?

4. Why is it encouraging to know that God's purposes never change?

5. God cannot lie. What kind of security does that give you?

INSPIRATION

In the barren prairie, the hiker huddles down. The cold northerly sweeps over him, stinging his face and numbing his fingers. The whistle of the wind is deafening. The hiker hugs his knees to his chest, yearning for warmth.

He doesn't move. The sky is orange with dirt. His teeth are grainy, his eyes sooty. He thinks of quitting. Going home. Home to the mountains.

"Ahh. The mountains." The spirit that moved him in the mountains seems so far away. For a moment, his mind wanders back to his homeland. Green country. Mountain trails. Fresh water. Hikers hiking on well marked trails. No surprises, few fears, rich companionship.

One day, while on a brisk hike, he had stopped to look out from the mountains across the neighboring desert. He felt strangely pulled to the sweeping barrenness that lay before him. The next day he paused again. And the next, and the next. "Shouldn't someone try to take life to the desert?" Slowly the flicker in his heart became a flame.

Many agreed that someone should go, but no one volunteered.

Uncharted land, fearful storms, loneliness.

But the hiker, spurred by the enthusiasm of others, determined to go. After careful preparation, he set out, alone. With the cheers of his friends behind him, he descended the grassy highlands and entered the desolate wilderness.

The first few days his steps were springy and his eye was keen. He yearned to do his part to bring life to the desert. Then came the heat. The scorpions. The monotony. The snakes. Slowly, the fire diminished. And now . . . the storm. The endless roar of the wind. The relentless, cursed cold.

"I don't know how much more I can take." Weary and beaten, the hiker considers going back. "At least I got this far." Knees tucked under him, head bowed, almost touching the ground. "Will it ever stop?"

Grimly he laughs at the irony of the situation. "Some hiker. Too tired to go on, yet too ashamed to go home." Deep, deep is the struggle. No longer can he hear the voices of friends. Long gone is the romance of his mission. No longer does he float on the fancifulness of a dream.

"Maybe someone else should do this. I'm too young, too inexperienced." The winds of discouragement and fear whip at his fire, exhausting what is left of the flame. But the coals remain, hidden and hot.

The hiker, now almost the storm's victim, looks one last time for the fire. (Is there any greater challenge than of stirring a spirit while in the clutches of defeat?) Yearning and clawing, the temptation to quit is gradually overcome by the urge to go on. Blowing on the coals, the hiker once again hears the call to the desert. Though faint, the call is clear.

With all the strength he can summon, the hiker rises to his feet, bows his head, and takes his first step into the wind. (From *Shaped by God* by Max Lucado)

REACTION

6. What is a Christian's primary goal in this life?

7. What obstacles stand in the way of your fulfilling this goal?

8. How can we prepare ourselves to face and overcome those obstacles?

9. What does it mean to trust God's promises?

10. What are the rewards of trusting God?

11. Which of God's promises will you remember this week to help you persevere?

LIFE LESSONS

Persevering in our walk with God can be tough. But we don't have to do it alone. The passage from this lesson reminds us of God's commitment to work in us and through us, much as the seed uses the soil to produce a great harvest. He kept his promise to Abraham; he will keep his promise to us. He specializes in using weak things to accomplish his plan and demonstrate his power. We are the weak things. God has made a promise backed up by his character. We may fail to trust God, but God will never fail to be trustworthy!

DEVOTION

Father, help us to maintain our promise of faithfulness to you, even in times when we are filled with doubt, fear, and insecurity. Give us great courage to endure the storms that come our way. Help us press on toward the goal you have set for us.

For more Bible passages about perseverance, see Acts 20:24; Romans 5:3–4; 1 Timothy 4:16; 2 Timothy 2:12; Hebrews 10:36; 12:1–3; James 1:2–4, 12; 5:11; 2 Peter 1:5–11; Revelation 2:2–3.

To complete the book of Hebrews during this twelve-part study, read Hebrews 6:1–7:28.

JOURNALING

What fears and doubts do I face today? How does this passage challenge me to deal with those feelings?

GOD FORGIVES AND FORGETS

MAX LUCADO

REFLECTION

Think of a time when you received forgiveness from a friend. Did you have to ask for it, or was forgiveness offered before you could even apologize? How did his/her forgiveness make you feel?

SITUATION

In Hebrews 5 and 7, the writer introduced Melchizedek, the mysterious Old Testament king and priest who was acknowledged by Abraham (Gen. 14:18–20). Melchizedek's priesthood was one of God's clues revealing his broader plan for the world. He served as a "type" or prefigure of Christ, who fulfilled the high priesthood. Jesus was now the central focus of God's covenant-agreement with his people, a far better covenant than even the great covenant God had established with Abraham and his descendants.

OBSERVATION

Read Hebrews 8:1–13 from the NCV or the NKJV.

NCV

¹Here is the point of what we are saying: We have a high priest who sits on the right side of God's throne in heaven. ²Our high priest serves in the Most Holy Place, the true place of worship that was made by God, not by humans.

³Every high priest has the work of offering gifts and sacrifices to God. So our high priest must also offer something to God. ⁴If our high priest were now living on earth, he would not be a priest, because there are already priests here who follow the law by offering gifts to God. ⁵The work they do as priests is only a copy and a shadow of what is in heaven. This is why God warned Moses when he was ready to build the Holy Tent: "Be very careful to make everything by the plan I showed you on the mountain." ⁶But the priestly work that has been given to Jesus is much greater than the work that was given to the other priests. In the same way, the new agreement that Jesus brought from God to his people is much greater than the old one. And the new agreement is based on promises of better things.

⁷If there had been nothing wrong with the first agreement, there would have been no need for a second agreement. ⁸But God found something wrong with his people. He says:

   "Look, the time is coming, says the LORD,
      when I will make a new agreement
      with the people of Israel
      and the people of Judah.
   ⁹It will not be like the agreement
   I made with their ancestors
      when I took them by the hand
      to bring them out of Egypt.
   But they broke that agreement,
      and I turned away from them, says the LORD.
   ¹⁰This is the agreement I will make
      with the people of Israel at that time, says the LORD.
   I will put my teachings in their minds and
      write them on their hearts.
   I will be their God,
      and they will be my people.
   ¹¹People will no longer have to teach their neighbors and relatives
      to know the Lord,
      because all people will know me,
      from the least to the most important.
   ¹²I will forgive them for the wicked things they did,
      and I will not remember their sins anymore."

¹³God called this a new agreement, so he has made the first agreement old. And anything that is old and worn out is ready to disappear.

NKJV

¹Now this is the main point of the things we are saying: We have such a High Priest, who is seated at the right hand of the throne of the Majesty in the heavens, ²a Minister of the sanctuary and of the true tabernacle which the Lord erected, and not man.

³For every high priest is appointed to offer both gifts and sacrifices. Therefore it is necessary that this One also have something to offer. ⁴For if He were on earth, He would not be a priest, since there are priests who offer the gifts according to the law; ⁵who serve the copy and shadow of the heavenly things, as Moses was divinely instructed when he was about to make the tabernacle. For He said, "See that you make all things according to the pattern shown you on the mountain." ⁶But now He has obtained a more excellent ministry, inasmuch as He is also Mediator of a better covenant, which was established on better promises.

⁷For if that first covenant had been faultless, then no place would have been sought for a second. ⁸Because finding fault with them, He says: "Behold, the days are coming, says the Lord, when I will make a new covenant with the house of Israel and with the house of Judah—⁹not according to the covenant that I made with their fathers in the day when I took them by the hand to lead them out of the land of Egypt; because they did not continue in My covenant, and I disregarded them, says the Lord. ¹⁰For this is the covenant that I will make with the house of Israel after those days, says the Lord: I will put My laws in their mind and write them on their hearts; and I will be their God, and they shall be My people. ¹¹None of them shall teach his neighbor, and none his brother, saying, 'Know the Lord,' for all shall know Me, from the least of them to the greatest of them. ¹²For I will be merciful to their unrighteousness, and their sins and their lawless deeds I will remember no more."

¹³In that He says, "A new covenant," He has made the first obsolete. Now what is becoming obsolete and growing old is ready to vanish away.

EXPLORATION

1. What are Jesus' duties as High Priest, and how does he fulfill them?

2. Why is Jesus' priestly work greater than the work of other priests?

3. How is the new covenant different from the old covenant?

4. Why did God establish a new agreement with his people?

5. What expanded promises did God make to his people under the new covenant?

INSPIRATION

I was thanking the Father today for his mercy. I began listing the sins he'd forgiven. One by one I thanked God for forgiving my stumbles and tumbles. My motives were pure and my heart was thankful, but my understanding of God was wrong. It was when I used the word "remember" that it hit me. . . .

God doesn't just forgive, he forgets. He erases the board. He destroys the evidence. He burns the microfilm. He clears the computer. . . .

No, he doesn't remember. But I do, you do. You still remember. You're like me. You still remember what you did before you changed. In the cellar of your heart lurk the ghosts of yesterday's sins. Sins you've confessed; errors of which you've repented; damage you've done your best to repair.

And though you're a different person, the ghosts still linger. Though you've locked the basement door, they still haunt you. They float to meet you, spooking your soul and robbing your joy. With wordless whispers they remind you of moments when you forgot whose child you were. . . .

Poltergeists from yesterday's pitfalls. Spiteful specters that slyly suggest, "Are you really forgiven? Sure, God forgets most of our mistakes, but do you think he could actually forget the time you . . ."

Was [God] exaggerating when he said he would cast our sins as far as the east is from the west? Do you actually believe he would make a statement like "I will not hold their iniquities against them" and then rub our noses in them whenever we ask for help?

You see, God is either the God of perfect grace, or he is not God. Grace forgets. Period. He who is perfect love cannot hold grudges. If he does, then he isn't perfect love. And if he isn't perfect love, you might as well put this book down and go fishing, because both of us are chasing fairy tales.

But I believe in his loving forgetfulness. And I believe he has a graciously terrible memory. (From *God Came Near* by Max Lucado)

REACTION

6. What do you usually expect when you ask a friend for forgiveness?

7. What can we expect from God when we confess our sins to him?

8. How can you remind yourself that God has forgiven you and does not hold your sin against you?

9. Why do we sometimes doubt God's forgiveness?

10. How can we find freedom from a false sense of guilt?

11. Why is it important for believers to express thanks to God for his forgiveness?

LIFE LESSONS

God not only shows himself willing to forgive and forget, but he also goes out of his way to extend the opportunity for confession and relationship. His covenant gives us permission to count on him. God is determined to fashion a people with whom to spend eternity, and no obstacle will prevent his plan. All the difficulties that must be overcome and all the hard work that must be done he has done for us. And he will hold none of it against us. We have his word: "I will remember no more."

DEVOTION

Thank you, Father, for your forgiveness and your gracious forgetfulness. Teach us to confess our sins quickly, to fully accept your forgiveness so that we can enjoy a restored relationship with you, and to release any feelings of guilt or self-condemnation. May we experience the joy and freedom your forgiveness brings.

For more Bible passages about God's forgiveness, see Numbers 14:18–20; 2 Chronicles 7:14; Nehemiah 9:17; Psalms 86:5; 103:3; Daniel 9:9; Micah 7:18; Matthew 6:12–14; Mark 2:5–12; Colossians 2:13–14; 3:13; 1 John 1:9.

To complete the book of Hebrews during this twelve-part study, read Hebrews 8:1–13.

JOURNALING

What past sins haunt me? How can I learn to forgive myself for the sins God has already forgiven?

LESSON SEVEN

A SACRIFICE
FOR SINS

MAX
LUCADO

REFLECTION

Imagine being at the scene of Jesus' crucifixion. Consider for a few moments exactly how you picture Jesus on the cross. Now think about your own point of observation. Where are you standing? Near? Far? Are you looking down or up at him? How does your point of view affect the way you respond? What does his suffering for you make you feel?

SITUATION

The book of Hebrews repeatedly sends us back to the Old Testament for understanding. The Bible puts Jesus in the center of history. God prepared the world for a long time before Jesus came. Jesus brought deep significance to the Old Testament rituals of worship and sacrifice that God had given to his people. They worshiped in a tent made of hands, the priest offered animal sacrifices for their sins on the altar, and God's presence was only accessible in the Most Holy Place behind the curtain. Our appreciation of Jesus' work on our behalf grows as we take time to understand the Old Testament background of God's actions.

OBSERVATION

Read Hebrews 9:11–28 from the NCV or the NKJV.

NCV

11But when Christ came as the high priest of the good things we now have, he entered the greater and more perfect tent. It is not made by humans and does not belong to this world. 12Christ entered the Most Holy Place only once—and for all time. He did not take with him the blood of goats and calves. His sacrifice was his own blood, and by it he set us free from sin forever. 13The blood of goats and bulls and the ashes of a cow are sprinkled on the people who are unclean, and this makes their bodies clean again. 14How much more is done by the blood of Christ. He offered himself through the eternal Spirit as a perfect sacrifice to God. His blood will make our consciences pure from useless acts so we may serve the living God.

15For this reason Christ brings a new agreement from God to his people. Those who are called by God can now receive the blessings he has promised, blessings that will last forever. They can have those things because Christ died so that the people who lived under the first agreement could be set free from sin.

16When there is a will, it must be proven that the one who wrote that will is dead. 17A will means nothing while the person is alive; it can be used only after the person dies. 18This is why even the first agreement could not begin without blood to show death. 19First, Moses told all the people every command in the law. Next he took the blood of calves and mixed it with water. Then he used red wool and a branch of the hyssop plant to sprinkle it on the book of the law and on all the people. 20He said, "This is the blood that begins the Agreement that God commanded you to obey." 21In the same way, Moses sprinkled the blood on the Holy Tent and over all the things used in worship. 22The law says that almost everything must be made clean by blood, and sins cannot be forgiven without blood to show death.

23So the copies of the real things in heaven had to be made clean by animal sacrifices. But the real things in heaven need much better sacrifices. 24Christ did not go into the Most Holy Place made by humans, which is only a copy of the real one. He went into heaven itself and is there now before God to help us. 25The high priest enters the Most Holy Place once every year with blood that is not his own. But Christ did not offer himself many times. 26Then he would have had to suffer many times since the world was made. But Christ came only once and for all time at just the right time to take away all sin by sacrificing himself. 27Just as everyone must die once and be judged, 28so Christ was offered as a sacrifice one time to take away the sins of many people. And he will come a second time, not to offer himself for sin, but to bring salvation to those who are waiting for him.

NKJV

11But Christ came as High Priest of the good things to come, with the greater and more perfect tabernacle not made with hands, that is, not of this creation. 12Not with the blood of goats and calves, but with His own blood He entered the Most Holy Place once for all, having obtained eternal redemption. 13For if the blood of bulls and goats and the ashes of a heifer, sprinkling the unclean, sanctifies for the purifying of the flesh, 14how much more shall the blood of Christ, who through the eternal Spirit offered Himself without spot to God, cleanse your conscience from dead works to serve the living God? 15And for this reason He is the Mediator of the new covenant, by means of death, for the redemption of the transgressions under the first covenant, that those who are called may receive the promise of the eternal inheritance.

16For where there is a testament, there must also of necessity be the death of the testator. 17For a testament is in force after men are dead, since it has no power at all while the testator lives. 18Therefore not even the first covenant was dedicated without blood. 19For when Moses had spoken every precept to all the people according to the law, he took the blood of calves and goats, with water, scarlet wool, and hyssop, and sprinkled both the book itself and all the people, 20saying, "This is the blood of the covenant which God has *commanded you." ²¹Then likewise he sprinkled with blood both the tabernacle and all the vessels of the ministry. ²²And according to the law almost all things are purified with blood, and without shedding of blood there is no remission.*

²³Therefore it was necessary that the copies of the things in the heavens should be purified with these, but the heavenly things themselves with better sacrifices than these. ²⁴For Christ has not entered the holy places made with hands, which are copies of the true, but into heaven itself, now to appear in the presence of God for us; ²⁵not that He should offer Himself often, as the high priest enters the Most Holy Place every year with blood of another—²⁶He then would have had to suffer often since the foundation of the world; but now, once at the end of the ages, He has appeared to put away sin by the sacrifice of Himself. ²⁷And as it is appointed for men to die once, but after this the judgment, ²⁸so Christ was offered once to bear the sins of many. To those who eagerly wait for Him He will appear a second time, apart from sin, for salvation.

EXPLORATION

1. How can people receive the blessings God has promised?

2. Why did Christ establish a new agreement between God and people?

3. Why is the shedding of blood necessary for the forgiveness of sins?

4. How does Christ's blood purify us?

5. How was Christ's sacrifice superior to the sacrifice of animals?

INSPIRATION

Several hundred feet beneath my chair is a lake, an underground cavern of crystalline water known as the Edwards Aquifer. We south-Texans know much about this aquifer. We know its length (175 miles). We know its layout (west to east except under San Antonio, where it runs north to south). We know the water is pure. Fresh. It irrigates farms and waters lawns and fills pools and quenches thirst. We know much about the aquifer.

But for all the facts we do know, there is an essential one we don't. We don't know its size. The depth of the cavern? A mystery. Number of gallons? Unmeasured. No one knows the amount of water the aquifer contains . . . Could this be? I decided to find out. I called a water conservationist. "That's right," he affirmed. "We estimate. We try to measure. But the exact quantity? No one knows." Remarkable.

Bring to mind another unmeasured pool? Not a pool of water but a pool of love. God's love. Aquifer fresh. Pure as April snow. One swallow slackens the thirsty throat and softens the crusty heart. Immerse a life in God's love, and watch it emerge cleansed and changed. We know the impact of God's love.

But the volume? No person has ever measured it.

Moral meteorologists, worried we might exhaust the supply, suggest otherwise. "Don't drink too deeply," they caution, recommending rationed portions. Some people, after all, drink more than their share. Terrorists and traitors and wife beaters—let such scoundrels start drinking, and they may take too much.

But who has plumbed the depths of God's love? Only God has. "Want to see the size of my love?" he invites. "Ascend the winding path outside of Jerusalem. Follow the dots of bloody dirt until you crest the hill. Before looking up, pause and hear me whisper, "This is how much I love you."

Whip-ripped muscles drape his back. Blood rivulets over his face. His eyes and lips are swollen shut. Pain rages at wildfire intensity. As he sinks to relieve the agony of his legs, his airway closes. At the edge of suffocation, he shoves pierced muscles against the spike and inches up the cross. He does this for hours. Painfully up and down until his strength and our doubts are gone.

Does God love you? Behold the cross, and behold your answer. (From *It's Not About Me* by Max Lucado)

REACTION

6. How do people try to make themselves right with God? What results from their efforts?

7. What can free us from the frustration of trying to earn God's approval?

8. What is significant about the fact that Christ died "once for all"?

9. How would you explain to an unbelieving friend why Jesus had to die?

10. How would your life be different if Christ had not died?

11. How can you thank Jesus today for sacrificing his life to save you?

LIFE LESSONS

Living in a world of choices, it isn't hard for us to assume that Jesus is optional. We can easily accept the suggestion that he is one good model among many good models. One great teacher in a long line of great teachers. A godly man, but surely not God. And yet the teaching of Hebrews brings us back to the stark truth. Jesus did something no one else could do, has done, or will do. He struck a bargain with God on our behalf. He served as sacrificial lamb and sacrificing priest. As the God-man, he did what no other human could do. His role for us isn't optional, but essential. We can reject it or accept it. But we dare not consider Jesus only an option.

DEVOTION

Because of your great love for us, Father, you sacrificed your only Son so that we could receive forgiveness for our sins and enjoy eternal life with you. We are thankful that you did not hold anything back in your plan to save us. Show us how to give ourselves completely to you in return.

For more Bible passages about Christ's sacrifice for sin, see John 1:29; Romans 3:22–27; 4:25; 6:23; 2 Corinthians 5:21; 2 Timothy 1:8–10; Hebrews 2:17; 7:27; 10:5–14; 1 John 1:7; 2:2; 4:10.

To complete the book of Hebrews during this twelve-part study, read Hebrews 9:1–28.

JOURNALING

What benefits and blessings do I enjoy because of Jesus' death on the cross?

LESSON EIGHT

CONFIDENCE
IN CHRIST

MAX
LUCADO

REFLECTION

Courage and boldness are often hidden traits, easier to claim than to display. They come out when they are necessary and not a moment sooner. God supplies courage. He produces boldness in people. Think of a time when God gave you courage or boldness. What happened? How did this affect your life?

SITUATION

Up to this point in the book of Hebrews, the writer has focused on teaching, explaining, and inspiring. Now he switches gears into practical illustrations and application. He reiterates to his readers that because they have been freed by Jesus' blood and sacrifice, it's time to act. It's time to step up or step aside. It's time to have confidence in Christ so that they might be bold with people.

OBSERVATION

Read Hebrews 10:19—39 from the NCV or the NKJV.

NCV

¹⁹*So, brothers and sisters, we are completely free to enter the Most Holy Place without fear because of the blood of Jesus' death. ²⁰We can enter through a new and living way that Jesus opened for us. It leads through the curtain—Christ's body. ²¹And since we have a great priest over God's house, ²²let us come near to God with a sincere heart and a sure faith, because we have been made free from a guilty conscience, and our bodies have been washed with pure water. ²³Let us hold firmly to the hope that we have confessed, because we can trust God to do what he promised.*

²⁴*Let us think about each other and help each other to show love and do good deeds. ²⁵You should not stay away from the church meetings, as some are doing, but you should meet together and encourage each other. Do this even more as you see the day coming.*

²⁶*If we decide to go on sinning after we have learned the truth, there is no longer any sacrifice for sins. ²⁷There is nothing but fear in waiting for the judgment and the terrible fire that will destroy all those who live against God. ²⁸Anyone who refused to obey the law of Moses was found guilty from the proof given by two or three witnesses. He was put to death without mercy. ²⁹So what do you think should be done to those who do not respect the Son of God, who look at the blood of the agreement that made them holy as no different from others' blood, who insult the Spirit of God's grace? Surely they should have a much worse punishment. ³⁰We know that God said, "I will punish those who do wrong; I will repay them." And he also said, "The Lord will judge his people." ³¹It is a terrible thing to fall into the hands of the living God.*

³²*Remember those days in the past when you first learned the truth. You had a hard struggle with many sufferings, but you continued strong. ³³Sometimes you were hurt and attacked before crowds of people, and sometimes you shared with those who were being treated that way. ³⁴You helped the prisoners. You even had joy when all that you owned was taken from you, because you knew you had something better and more lasting.*

³⁵*So do not lose the courage you had in the past, which has a great reward. ³⁶You must hold on, so you can do what God wants and receive what he has promised. ³⁷For in a very short time,*

> *"The One who is coming will come*
>   *and will not be delayed.*
> ³⁸*The person who is right with me*
>   *will live by trusting in me.*
> *But if he turns back with fear,*
>   *I will not be pleased with him."*

39But we are not those who turn back and are lost. We are people who have faith and are saved.

NKJV

19Therefore, brethren, having boldness to enter the Holiest by the blood of Jesus, 20by a new and living way which He consecrated for us, through the veil, that is, His flesh, 21and having a High Priest over the house of God, 22let us draw near with a true heart in full assurance of faith, having our hearts sprinkled from an evil conscience and our bodies washed with pure water. 23Let us hold fast the confession of our hope without wavering, for He who promised is faithful. 24And let us consider one another in order to stir up love and good works, 25not forsaking the assembling of ourselves together, as is the manner of some, but exhorting one another, and so much the more as you see the Day approaching.

26For if we sin willfully after we have received the knowledge of the truth, there no longer remains a sacrifice for sins, 27but a certain fearful expectation of judgment, and fiery indignation which will devour the adversaries. 28Anyone who has rejected Moses' law dies without mercy on the testimony of two or three witnesses. 29Of how much worse punishment, do you suppose, will he be thought worthy who has trampled the Son of God underfoot, counted the blood of the covenant by which he was sanctified a common thing, and insulted the Spirit of grace? 30For we know Him who said, "Vengeance is Mine, I will repay," says the Lord. And again, "The LORD will judge His people." 31It is a fearful thing to fall into the hands of the living God.

32But recall the former days in which, after you were illuminated, you endured a great struggle with sufferings: 33partly while you were made a spectacle both by reproaches and tribulations, and partly while you became companions of those who were so treated; 34for you had compassion on me in my chains, and joyfully accepted the plundering of your goods, knowing that you have a better and an enduring possession for yourselves in heaven. 35Therefore do not cast away your confidence, which has great reward. 36For you have need of endurance, so that after you have done the will of God, you may receive the promise:

> *37"For yet a little while,*
>
> *And He who is coming will come and will not tarry.*
>
> *38Now the just shall live by faith;*
>
> *But if anyone draws back,*
>
> *My soul has no pleasure in him."*

39But we are not of those who draw back to perdition, but of those who believe to the saving of the soul.

EXPLORATION

1. What gives believers confidence to approach a holy God?

2. List some of the opportunities and privileges Christ's death provides you.

3. What happens when people reject God's salvation?

4. What warnings does this passage give to people who turn away from their faith in Jesus?

5. The author of Hebrews said that it is a terrible thing to fall into the hands of the living God. What did he mean?

INSPIRATION

Imagine that you are an ice skater in competition. You are in first place with one more round to go. If you perform well, the trophy is yours. You are nervous, anxious, and frightened.

Then, only minutes before your performance, your trainer rushes to you with the thrilling news: "You've already won! The judges tabulated the scores, and the person in second place can't catch you. You are too far ahead."

Upon hearing that news, how will you feel? Exhilarated!

And how will you skate? Timidly? Cautiously? Of course not. How about courageously and confidently? You bet you will. You will do your best because the prize is yours. You will skate like a champion because that is what you are! You will hear the applause of victory . . .

The point is clear: the truth will triumph. The father of truth will win, and the followers of truth will be saved. (From *The Applause of Heaven* by Max Lucado)

REACTION

6. How does Jesus' victory over death affect your courage?

7. How should our confidence in Christ's ultimate victory change the way we live?

8. How can believers help one another to show love and do good deeds?

9. What can we gain from remembering the days when we were new believers?

10. Who is someone you can encourage to persevere through difficult times? What can you do for that person?

11. How can you depend more on other believers to help you grow in your faith and commitment to God?

LIFE LESSONS

Confidence flows out of our intimacy with and sure knowledge of Christ. We are to "enter" and "draw near" because we know Christ's love, because we know what he has done, and because those facts are sinking deeper and deeper into us. We practice boldness when we consider how to "stir up love and good works" in others. We grow in confidence when we persist in spending time with other believers, encouraging and accepting encouragement. We have to go beyond knowing that the "just live by faith" all the way to living by faith ourselves.

DEVOTION

Father, rekindle the fire that burned bright in our hearts when we first discovered your love and forgiveness. Renew our commitment to you and your work. Help us to be busy about the right business—the business of serving you.

For more Bible passages about Christ's victory over death, see John 16:33; 1 Corinthians 15:24–26, 54–58; 1 John 5:4; Revelation 3:21; 17:14.

To complete the book of Hebrews during this twelve-part study, read Hebrews 10:1–39.

JOURNALING

Do I still have the enthusiasm and commitment I had when I first became a Christian? How can I reenergize my devotion to Christ?

LESSON NINE

FAITH IN
GOD'S
PROMISES

MAX
LUCADO

REFLECTION

Make a list of three people who have taught you the most about how to live by faith. Think of a time when you have been memorably inspired by their faith in God. What was it that inspired you? How?

SITUATION

The writer of Hebrews loved the history of his people. He appreciated the way God had worked through his chosen people despite their many shortcomings. And, as chapter 11 brilliantly illustrates, he knew that God had worked through people of faith down through the centuries to keep his great plan on track. In compiling their names, the writer created what has come to be known as the Bible's Hall of Faith.

OBSERVATION

Read Hebrews 11:1–16 from the NCV or the NKJV.

NCV

¹Faith means being sure of the things we hope for and knowing that something is real even if we do not see it. ²Faith is the reason we remember great people who lived in the past.

³It is by faith we understand that the whole world was made by God's command so what we see was made by something that cannot be seen.

⁴It was by faith that Abel offered God a better sacrifice than Cain did. God said he was pleased with the gifts Abel offered and called Abel a good man because of his faith. Abel died, but through his faith he is still speaking.

⁵It was by faith that Enoch was taken to heaven so he would not die. He could not be found, because God had taken him away. Before he was taken, the Scripture says that he was a man who truly pleased God. ⁶Without faith no one can please God. Anyone who comes to God must believe that he is real and that he rewards those who truly want to find him.

⁷It was by faith that Noah heard God's warnings about things he could not yet see. He obeyed God and built a large boat to save his family. By his faith, Noah showed that the world was wrong, and he became one of those who are made right with God through faith.

⁸It was by faith Abraham obeyed God's call to go to another place God promised to give him. He left his own country, not knowing where he was to go. ⁹It was by faith that he lived like a foreigner in the country God promised to give him. He lived in tents with Isaac and Jacob, who had received that same promise from God. ¹⁰Abraham was waiting for the city that has real foundations—the city planned and built by God.

¹¹He was too old to have children, and Sarah could not have children. It was by faith that Abraham was made able to become a father, because he trusted God to do what he had promised. ¹²This man was so old he was almost dead, but from him came as many descendants as there are stars in the sky. Like the sand on the seashore, they could not be counted.

¹³All these great people died in faith. They did not get the things that God promised his people, but they saw them coming far in the future and were glad. They said they were like visitors and strangers on earth. ¹⁴When people say such things, they show they are looking for a country that will be their own. ¹⁵If they had been thinking about the country they had left, they could have gone back. ¹⁶But they were waiting for a better country—a heavenly country. So God is not ashamed to be called their God, because he has prepared a city for them.

NKJV

¹Now faith is the substance of things hoped for, the evidence of things not seen. ²For by it the elders obtained a good testimony.

³By faith we understand that the worlds were framed by the word of God, so that the things which are seen were not made of things which are visible.

⁴By faith Abel offered to God a more excellent sacrifice than Cain, through which he obtained witness that he was righteous, God testifying of his gifts; and through it he being dead still speaks.

⁵By faith Enoch was taken away so that he did not see death, "and was not found, because God had taken him"; for before he was taken he had this testimony, that he pleased God. ⁶But without faith it is impossible to please Him, for he who comes to God must believe that He is, and that He is a rewarder of those who diligently seek Him.

⁷By faith Noah, being divinely warned of things not yet seen, moved with godly fear, prepared an ark for the saving of his household, by which he condemned the world and became heir of the righteousness which is according to faith.

⁸By faith Abraham obeyed when he was called to go out to the place which he would receive as an inheritance. And he went out, not knowing where he was going. ⁹By faith he dwelt in the land of promise as in a foreign country, dwelling in tents with Isaac and Jacob, the heirs with him of the same promise; ¹⁰for he waited for the city which has foundations, whose builder and maker is God.

¹¹By faith Sarah herself also received strength to conceive seed, and she bore a child when she was past the age, because she judged Him faithful who had promised. ¹²Therefore from one man, and him as good as dead, were born as many as the stars of the sky in multitude—innumerable as the sand which is by the seashore.

¹³These all died in faith, not having received the promises, but having seen them afar off were assured of them, embraced them and confessed that they were strangers and pilgrims on the earth. ¹⁴For those who say such things declare plainly that they seek a homeland. ¹⁵And truly if they had called to mind that country from which they had come out, they would have had opportunity to return. ¹⁶But now they desire a better, that is, a heavenly country. Therefore God is not ashamed to be called their God, for He has prepared a city for them.

EXPLORATION

1. Why should we remember people of faith who lived in the past?

2. What made the faith of these people extraordinary?

3. How did these people demonstrate their faith in God?

4. Why did these people say they were like visitors and strangers on earth (v. 13)?

5. How can God's people today show their trust in his promises?

INSPIRATION

Faith is the belief that God is real and that God is good. Faith is not a mystical experience or a midnight vision or a voice in the forest . . . It is a choice to believe that the one who made it all hasn't left it all and that he still sends light into the shadows and responds to gestures of faith . . .

Faith is not the belief that God will do what you want. Faith is the belief that God will do what is right.

"Blessed are the dirt-poor, nothing-to-give, trapped-in-a-corner, destitute, diseased," Jesus said, "for theirs is the kingdom of heaven" (Matt. 5:6, my translation).

God's economy is upside down (or right side up and ours is upside down!). God says that the more hopeless your circumstances, the more likely your salvation. The greater your cares, the more genuine your prayers. The darker the room, the greater the need for light. God's help is near and always available, but it is only given to those who seek it. Nothing results from apathy . . .

Compared to God's part, our part is minuscule but necessary. We don't have to do much, but we do have to do something. Write a letter. Ask forgiveness. Call a counselor. Confess. Call Mom. Visit a doctor. Be baptized. Feed a hungry person. Pray. Teach. Go.

Do something that demonstrates faith. For faith with no effort is no faith at all. God will respond. He has never rejected a genuine gesture of faith. Never. (From *He Still Moves Stones* by Max Lucado)

REACTION

6. Why is it impossible to please God without faith?

7. How do faith and obedience work together?

8. How does God respond to our faith?

9. What encouragement does this passage offer to people who have not had their prayers answered?

10. How has your faith in God changed your perspective or goals in life?

11. What can you do to exercise faith this week?

LIFE LESSONS

We use casual faith in a thousand ways every day without thinking about it. Every time we sit in a chair, drive a car, eat a bite of food, we are exercising trust. We can't prove that the chair will hold us or that the car is safe or that the food isn't poisonous. We simply practice unintentional faith. That's not the kind of faith God expects from us. The examples of faith we have seen in this lesson show us *intentional* faith. Faith that God is there and is active in our lives. Faith that doesn't know the immediate outcome but trusts God anyway. Faith that suffers because it knows that there's more at stake than the immediate situation. Faith that doesn't really expect everything to work out on this side of eternity. This is the faith that pleases God.

DEVOTION

Father, our faith is so weak. Forgive us for doubting you. Help us to persevere even when we haven't seen all of your promises fulfilled. Remind us that we are just passing through this life by focusing our eyes on a better country—our heavenly home.

For more Bible passages about faith, see 2 Chronicles 20:20; Isaiah 7:9; Matthew 21:21–22; John 8:30; Acts 15:8–9; Romans 1:17; 5:1–2; 1 Corinthians 16:13; Galatians 2:15–16; 3:22–27; Hebrews 4:14; 10:38; James 2:14–26; 1 Peter 1:8–9; Jude 1:3, 20.

To complete the book of Hebrews during this twelve-part study, read Hebrews 11:1–40.

JOURNALING

What specific things have happened in my life that remind me of God's faithfulness?

SUFFERING SERVES A PURPOSE

MAX LUCADO

REFLECTION

Good coaches explain their expectations, demonstrate what they demand, and insist on letting their players do it for themselves. Why? Because real learning on the court or field involves mistakes and pain. The same is true in life. The most valuable lessons in life are often remembered by the pain that was suffered in learning them. Think of a time when you endured something painful because you knew it would ultimately benefit you. What was your experience, and how did you benefit?

SITUATION

The amazing roll call of great people of the faith was inspiring. The writer could have just encouraged us to follow Moses' or Abraham's example. But he wasn't done. There was another name to mention, a name above all others. The other names were a memorial to great faith in the past; the last name is "the author and finisher of our faith." He is our example of how to endure suffering by looking beyond it.

OBSERVATION

Read Hebrews 12:1–11 from the NCV or the NKJV.

NCV

1We have around us many people whose lives tell us what faith means. So let us run the race that is before us and never give up. We should remove from our lives anything that would get in the way and the sin that so easily holds us back. 2Let us look only to Jesus, the One who began our faith and who makes it perfect. He suffered death on the cross. But he accepted the shame as if it were nothing because of the joy that God put before him. And now he is sitting at the right side of God's throne. 3Think about Jesus' example. He held on while wicked people were doing evil things to him. So do not get tired and stop trying.

4You are struggling against sin, but your struggles have not yet caused you to be killed. 5You have forgotten the encouraging words that call you his children:

> *"My child, don't think the Lord's discipline is worth nothing,*
>
> > *and don't stop trying when he corrects you.*
>
> *6The Lord disciplines those he loves,*
>
> > *and he punishes everyone he accepts as his child."*

7So hold on through your sufferings, because they are like a father's discipline. God is treating you as children. All children are disciplined by their fathers. 8If you are never disciplined (and every child must be disciplined), you are not true children. 9We have all had fathers here on earth who disciplined us, and we respected them. So it is even more important that we accept discipline from the Father of our spirits so we will have life. 10Our fathers on earth disciplined us for a short time in the way they thought was best. But God disciplines us to help us, so we can become holy as he is. 11We do not enjoy being disciplined. It is painful, but later, after we have learned from it, we have peace, because we start living in the right way.

NKJV

1Therefore we also, since we are surrounded by so great a cloud of witnesses, let us lay aside every weight, and the sin which so easily ensnares us, and let us run with endurance the race that is set before us, 2looking unto Jesus, the author and finisher of our faith, who for the joy that was set before Him endured the cross, despising the shame, and has sat down at the right hand of the throne of God.

3For consider Him who endured such hostility from sinners against Himself, lest you become weary and discouraged in your souls. 4You have not yet resisted to bloodshed, striving against sin. 5And you have forgotten the exhortation which speaks to you as to sons:

"My son, do not despise the chastening of the LORD,

Nor be discouraged when you are rebuked by Him;

6For whom the LORD *loves He chastens,*

And scourges every son whom He receives."

7If you endure chastening, God deals with you as with sons; for what son is there whom a father does not chasten? 8But if you are without chastening, of which all have become partakers, then you are illegitimate and not sons. 9Furthermore, we have had human fathers who corrected us, and we paid them respect. Shall we not much more readily be in subjection to the Father of spirits and live? 10For they indeed for a few days chastened us as seemed best to them, but He for our profit, that we may be partakers of His holiness. 11Now no chastening seems to be joyful for the present, but painful; nevertheless, afterward it yields the peaceable fruit of righteousness to those who have been trained by it.

EXPLORATION

1. Why did Jesus accept the shame of the cross?

2. What advice does this passage offer to those who are suffering?

3. Whom does God discipline, and where does suffering fit in?

4. Why does God allow his children to suffer?

5. Why is it important to accept God's discipline? Think about the difference between discipline as punishment and discipline as training.

INSPIRATION

He looked around the carpentry shop. He stood for a moment in the refuge of the little room that housed so many sweet memories. He balanced the hammer in his hand. He ran his fingers across the sharp teeth of the saw. He stroked the smoothly worn wood of the sawhorse. He had come to say goodbye.

It was time for him to leave. He had heard something that made him know it was time to go. So he came one last time to smell the sawdust and lumber.

Life was peaceful here. Life was so . . . safe . . .

I wonder if he wanted to stay . . . I wonder because I know he had already read the last chapter. He knew that the feet that would step out of the safe shadow of the carpentry shop would not rest until they'd been pierced and placed on a Roman cross . . .

If there was any hesitation on the part of his humanity, it was overcome by the compassion of his divinity. His divinity heard the voices . . . And his divinity saw the faces . . . From the face of Adam to the face of the infant born somewhere in the world as you read these words, he saw them all.

And you can be sure of one thing. Among the voices that found their way into that carpentry shop in Nazareth was your voice . . . Not only did he hear you, he saw you. He saw your face aglow the hour you first knew him. He saw your face in shame the hour you first fell. The same face that looked back at you from this morning's mirror, looked at him. And it was enough to kill him.

He left because of you.

He laid his security down with his hammer. He hung tranquility on the peg with his nail apron. He closed the window shutters on the sunshine of his youth and locked the door on the comfort and ease of anonymity.

Since he could bear your sins more easily than he could bear the thought of your hopelessness, he chose to leave. It wasn't easy. Leaving the carpentry shop never has been. (From *God Came Near* by Max Lucado)

REACTION

6. How can thinking about Jesus' suffering help you face the pain in your life?

7. In what specific ways does God discipline us?

8. How can we learn to recognize and respond to God's correction in our lives?

9. How does this passage challenge your attitude toward God's discipline?

10. What might God be teaching you through some present difficulties?

11. Why is it important to remember that God loves you even though he disciplines you?

LIFE LESSONS

We often miss the best lessons and benefits of discipline because we insist on thinking of it primarily as punishment rather than training. We fail to see God's purposes in the "race set before us" so we don't approach it the way Jesus approached the "joy set before him." One of the best exercises to break out of the resentment habit when it comes to discipline is to take a different tack: question the good stuff. It's easy to question pain and suffering, "Why me?" But how often do we question God's continual blessings, goodness, mercy, and kindness? How often do we say, "Why did I have such a good day today?" or "Lord, why did you supply that need today?" God has a purpose in everything that comes our way, whether it's suffering or grace.

DEVOTION

Father, forgive us for the times we have shaken our heads and pounded our fists against the earth and cried, "Why, God?" For, Father, we know that when you allow us to suffer, you have our best interests at heart. Teach us to submit to your will instead of fighting for our own way. And in our darkest moments, remind us that you still love us.

For more Bible passages about God's discipline, see Deuteronomy 4:36; 11:2–7; Job 5:17; Psalm 94:12; Proverbs 3:11; 10:17; Jeremiah 30:11; Hosea 5:1–2; Revelation 3:19.

To complete the book of Hebrews during this twelve-part study, read Hebrews 12:1–11.

JOURNALING

How has God's discipline improved my life and made me a more mature believer?

THE FEAR OF
THE LORD

MAX
LUCADO

REFLECTION

Think of a person you greatly admire. Would you find it easy to talk with that person, or do you just admire him from a distance? Would you be nervous or thrilled if he approached you? How do you show your respect for that person? Think about the connection between admiration, honor, and fear. What are your observations?

SITUATION

Following hard on the heels of enlightening and encouraging words about God's discipline in our lives, the writer urges the Hebrew Christians to live out what they know. Using the Old Testament imagery of God on Mount Sinai, he reminds them that we serve an awesome God and we are headed to an awesome heavenly city.

OBSERVATION

Read Hebrews 12:12–29 from the NCV or the NKJV.

NCV

12You have become weak, so make yourselves strong again. 13Live in the right way so that you will be saved and your weakness will not cause you to be lost.

14Try to live in peace with all people, and try to live free from sin. Anyone whose life is not holy will never see the Lord. 15Be careful that no one fails to receive God's grace and begins to cause trouble among you. A person like that can ruin many of you. 16Be careful that no one takes part in sexual sin or is like Esau and never thinks about God. As the oldest son, Esau would have received everything from his father, but he sold all that for a single meal. 17You remember that after Esau did this, he wanted to get his father's blessing, but his father refused. Esau could find no way to change what he had done, even though he wanted the blessing so much that he cried.

18You have not come to a mountain that can be touched and that is burning with fire. You have not come to darkness, sadness, and storms. 19You have not come to the noise of a trumpet or to the sound of a voice like the one the people of Israel heard and begged not to hear another word. 20They did not want to hear the command: "If anything, even an animal, touches the mountain, it must be put to death with stones." 21What they saw was so terrible that Moses said, "I am shaking with fear."

22But you have come to Mount Zion, to the city of the living God, the heavenly Jerusalem. You have come to thousands of angels gathered together with joy. 23You have come to the meeting of God's firstborn children whose names are written in heaven. You have come to God, the judge of all people, and to the spirits of good people who have been made perfect. 24You have come to Jesus, the One who brought the new agreement from God to his people, and you have come to the sprinkled blood that has a better message than the blood of Abel.

25So be careful and do not refuse to listen when God speaks. Others refused to listen to him when he warned them on earth, and they did not escape. So it will be worse for us if we refuse to listen to God who warns us from heaven. 26When he spoke before, his voice shook the earth, but now he has promised, "Once again I will shake not only the earth but also the heavens." 27The words "once again" clearly show us that everything that was made—things that can be shaken—will be destroyed. Only the things that cannot be shaken will remain.

28So let us be thankful, because we have a kingdom that cannot be shaken. We should worship God in a way that pleases him with respect and fear, 29because our God is like a fire that burns things up.

NKJV

12Therefore strengthen the hands which hang down, and the feeble knees, 13and make straight paths for your feet, so that what is lame may not be dislocated, but rather be healed.

14Pursue peace with all people, and holiness, without which no one will see the Lord: 15looking carefully lest anyone fall short of the grace of God; lest any root of bitterness springing up cause trouble, and by this many become defiled; 16lest there be any fornicator or profane person like Esau, who for one morsel of food sold his birthright. 17For you know that afterward, when he wanted to inherit the blessing, he was rejected, for he found no place for repentance, though he sought it diligently with tears.

18For you have not come to the mountain that may be touched and that burned with fire, and to blackness and darkness and tempest, 19and the sound of a trumpet and the voice of words, so that those who heard it begged that the word should not be spoken to them anymore. 20(For they could not endure what was commanded: "And if so much as a beast touches the mountain, it shall be stoned or shot with an arrow." ²¹And so terrifying was the sight that Moses said, "I am exceedingly afraid and trembling.")

²²But you have come to Mount Zion and to the city of the living God, the heavenly Jerusalem, to an innumerable company of angels, ²³to the general assembly and church of the firstborn who are registered in heaven, to God the Judge of all, to the spirits of just men made perfect, ²⁴to Jesus the Mediator of the new covenant, and to the blood of sprinkling that speaks better things than that of Abel.

²⁵See that you do not refuse Him who speaks. For if they did not escape who refused Him who spoke on earth, much more shall we not escape if we turn away from Him who speaks from heaven, ²⁶whose voice then shook the earth; but now He has promised, saying, "Yet once more I shake not only the earth, but also heaven." ²⁷Now this, "Yet once more," indicates the removal of those things that are being shaken, as of things that are made, that the things which cannot be shaken may remain.

²⁸Therefore, since we are receiving a kingdom which cannot be shaken, let us have grace, by which we may serve God acceptably with reverence and godly fear. ²⁹For our God is a consuming fire.

EXPLORATION

1. Why should Christians "live in the right way"?

2. How can Christians avoid Esau's mistake?

3. What difference has Jesus made in the way people know God?

4. What will remain after God destroys this world?

5. What kind of worship pleases God?

INSPIRATION

"When they saw who he was, he disappeared. They said to each other, 'It felt like a fire burning in us when Jesus talked to us on the road and explained the Scriptures to us'" (Luke 24:31–32 NCV).

Don't you love that verse? They knew they had been with Jesus because of the fire within them. God reveals his will by setting a torch in your soul. He gave Jeremiah a fire for hard hearts. He gave Nehemiah a fire for a forgotten city. He set Abraham on fire for a land he'd never seen. He set Isaiah on fire with a vision he couldn't resist. Forty years of fruitless preaching didn't extinguish the fire of Noah. Forty years of wilderness wandering didn't douse the passion of Moses. Jericho couldn't slow Joshua, and Goliath didn't deter David. There was a fire within them.

And isn't there one within you? Want to know God's will for your life? Then answer this question: What ignites your heart? Forgotten orphans? Untouched nations? The inner city? The outer limits?

Heed the fire within!

Do you have a passion to sing? Then sing!

Are you stirred to manage? Then manage!

Do you ache for the ill? Then treat them!

Do you hurt for the lost? Then teach them!

As a young man I felt the call to preach. Unsure if I was correct in my reading of God's will for me, I sought the counsel of a minister I admired. His counsel still rings true. "Don't preach," he said, "unless you have to."

As I pondered his words I found my answer: "I *have* to. If I don't, the fire will consume me."

What is the fire that consumes you?

Mark it down: Jesus comes to set you on fire! He walks as a torch from heart to heart, warming the cold and thawing the chilled and stirring the ashes. He is at once a Galilean wildfire and a welcome candle. He comes to purge infection and illuminate your direction.

The fire of your heart is the light of your path. Disregard it at your own expense. Fan it at your own delight. Blow it. Stir it. Nourish it. Cynics will doubt it. Those without it will mock it. But those who know it—those who know *him*—will understand it.

To meet the Savior is to be set aflame. To discover the flame is to discover his will. And to discover his will is to access a world like none you've ever seen. (From *The Great House of God* by Max Lucado)

REACTION

6. What does Scripture mean when it compares God to "a fire that burns things up"?

7. What does it mean to fear God?

8. How does the fear of the Lord affect your daily life?

9. What can we learn about our future from this passage?

10. If this world will be destroyed, how should we spend our time and energy?

11. What does the way you spend your time reveal about your view of God?

LIFE LESSONS

God, who came to us in Jesus Christ, is certainly worthy to be feared—as in literally provoking terror. But he welcomes us to approach him in another kind of fear—awe, honor, respect, and trust. Our capacity to appreciate what God has done in us and what he will do through us always flows from our fear of God. Read again the quote from *The Great House of God* (page 106). Fearing God leads to serving him. The *how* of doing God's will comes through our continual exposure to God's Word and God's Spirit. The *what* of doing God's will comes mostly from within, recognizing the way God has put us together and trusting his purposes in how we are wired.

DEVOTION

Dear Father, teach us what it means to worship you in reverence and awe. Purify us and make us holy as we eagerly wait for your unshakable kingdom to come to earth. Help us to see what is important, what is eternal, and what is lasting.

For more Bible passages about fearing God, see Deuteronomy 6:13; 31:12–13; 1 Samuel 12:14–15; 2 Chronicles 19:7; Psalms 2:11; 19:9; 90:11; 147:11; Proverbs 1:7; 8:13; 10:27; Ecclesiastes 12:13–14; Isaiah 33:6; Luke 12:5; 2 Corinthians 5:11; Revelation 14:7.

To complete the book of Hebrews during this twelve-part study, read Hebrews 12:12–29.

JOURNALING

How can I demonstrate reverence for God?

LESSON TWELVE

SERVING
OTHERS

MAX
LUCADO

REFLECTION

Jesus described his whole purpose for coming to earth as being one of *service*. He came to serve. He told his disciples on his last night with them before his death, "If I then, your Lord and Teacher, have washed your feet, you also ought to wash one another's feet. For I have given you an example, that you should do as I have done to you" (John 13:14–15 NKJV). When has a Christian brother or sister served you in a meaningful way? How did this affect you?

SITUATION

The writer of Hebrews devotes his final words to a theme he touched on repeatedly throughout the letter: love and service. He encourages his brothers and sisters in Christ with a fervent appeal to see every relationship and every situation primarily as an opportunity to serve in the name of Christ.

OBSERVATION

Read Hebrews 13:1–16 from the NCV or the NKJV.

NCV

¹Keep on loving each other as brothers and sisters. ²Remember to welcome strangers, because some who have done this have welcomed angels without knowing it. ³Remember those who are in prison as if you were in prison with them. Remember those who are suffering as if you were suffering with them.

⁴Marriage should be honored by everyone, and husband and wife should keep their marriage pure. God will judge as guilty those who take part in sexual sins. ⁵Keep your lives free from the love of money, and be satisfied with what you have. God has said,

> *"I will never leave you;*
>
> *I will never forget you."*

⁶So we can be sure when we say,

> *"I will not be afraid, because the Lord is my helper.*
>
> *People can't do anything to me."*

⁷*Remember your leaders who taught God's message to you. Remember how they lived and died, and copy their faith.* ⁸*Jesus Christ is the same yesterday, today, and forever.*

⁹*Do not let all kinds of strange teachings lead you into the wrong way. Your hearts should be strengthened by God's grace, not by obeying rules about foods, which do not help those who obey them.*

¹⁰*We have a sacrifice, but the priests who serve in the Holy Tent cannot eat from it.* ¹¹*The high priest carries the blood of animals into the Most Holy Place where he offers this blood for sins. But the bodies of the animals are burned outside the camp.* ¹²*So Jesus also suffered outside the city to make his people holy with his own blood.* ¹³*So let us go to Jesus outside the camp, holding on as he did when we are abused.*

¹⁴*Here on earth we do not have a city that lasts forever, but we are looking for the city that we will have in the future.* ¹⁵*So through Jesus let us always offer to God our sacrifice of praise, coming from lips that speak his name.* ¹⁶*Do not forget to do good to others, and share with them, because such sacrifices please God.*

NKJV

¹*Let brotherly love continue.* ²*Do not forget to entertain strangers, for by so doing some have unwittingly entertained angels.* ³*Remember the prisoners as if chained with them—those who are mistreated—since you yourselves are in the body also.*

⁴*Marriage is honorable among all, and the bed undefiled; but fornicators and adulterers God will judge.*

⁵*Let your conduct be without covetousness; be content with such things as you have. For He Himself has said, "I will never leave you nor forsake you."* ⁶*So we may boldly say:*

> *"The LORD is my helper;*
>
> *I will not fear.*
>
> *What can man do to me?"*

⁷*Remember those who rule over you, who have spoken the word of God to you, whose faith follow, considering the outcome of their conduct.* ⁸*Jesus Christ is the same yesterday, today, and forever.* ⁹*Do not be carried about with various and strange doctrines. For it is good that the heart be established by grace, not with foods which have not profited those who have been occupied with them.*

¹⁰*We have an altar from which those who serve the tabernacle have no right to eat.* ¹¹*For the bodies of those animals, whose blood is brought into the sanctuary by the high priest for sin, are burned outside the camp.* ¹²*Therefore Jesus also, that He might sanctify the people with His own blood, suffered outside the gate.* ¹³*Therefore let us go forth to Him, outside the camp, bearing His reproach.* ¹⁴*For here we have no continuing city, but we seek the one to come.* ¹⁵*Therefore by Him let us continually offer the sacrifice of praise to God, that is, the fruit of our lips, giving thanks to His name.* ¹⁶*But do not forget to do good and to share, for with such sacrifices God is well pleased.*

EXPLORATION

1. How should Christians show their love for one another?

2. What responsibility do believers have to help people in need? Why?

3. What gives believers a sense of satisfaction and contentment?

4. What is the future city described in this passage, and what is the writer's purpose in bringing it up?

5. What kind of sacrifices please God?

INSPIRATION

Two great problems in serving others are both problems of human nature, of focusing on our relationship with people instead of our relationship with Christ. The first problem is that people will expect too much of you; and the second, you will expect too much of them. Both of these problems are problems of unrealistic expectations. Expectations must be focused on Christ, not each other. He is the only One who will consistently not let us down.

The milk of human sympathy will undernourish your soul. No amount of human gratitude will properly compensate your effort to improve the human condition. When we focus on serving the person, we are inevitably disappointed. And what's more, we will disappoint them. Serving people for the sake of their gratitude is a guaranteed formula for disappointment. Just when you begin to feel good about your labors, someone lets you down. Or, more likely, someone will expect too much from you and accuse you of letting them down. Either way, your destiny is to be terribly discouraged. . . .

The key is the personal relationship with Christ. The focus must not be on serving others or on being served. The focus must be on Jesus, on becoming so absorbed in the relationship with Him that every other thing is a response to our relationship. We don't serve men; we serve God. Have no expectations of men. Focus on the personal relationship with Him, and there will be an overflow available for others.

Look to Christ alone for gratitude. If you serve Christ, then you will remember to look to Him for your approval, not to the milk of human sympathy. He will reward you for serving others; in fact, He is the reward . . . The personal relationship with Christ is the oasis in the desert of human relations. When people begin to wear you down, let it remind you that you are not in the overflow. It is time to drink of Christ. (From *Walking with Christ in the Details of Life* by Patrick Morley)

REACTION

6. How has your relationship with Jesus changed the way you treat others?

7. What problems arise in serving others?

8. How can we avoid or deal with these problems?

9. What is the key to enjoying Christian service?

10. What can you do when you feel discouraged about your ministry?

11. How can you remind yourself to seek only Christ's approval for your service?

LIFE LESSONS

The letter to the Hebrews began with a tribute to God's ultimate word spoken in and through Jesus Christ. The letter ends with a tribute to God's ultimate work in raising the "Lord Jesus from the dead" (13:20 NKJV). God said what had to be said and did what needed to be done. His desire is to make us "complete in every good work to do His will" (13:21 NKJV). The author has helped us look back at the Old Testament, not with the intention of reliving those days but to help us live in these days. God filled the history of his people with lessons that illuminate his magnificent plan for all people. Through the words of Hebrews we hear the voices of the ages, urging us to keep the faith in our times.

DEVOTION

Father, thank you for the perfect example of Christ's humble service. Keep our eyes focused on you, and protect us from selfish desires, ulterior motives, and unrealistic expectations. May your great love for us spur us on to love and serve one another.

For more Bible passages about serving, see Deuteronomy 10:12; 2 Chronicles 19:9; Psalm 2:11; Luke 12:35; 1 Corinthians 12:5; 16:15–16; 2 Corinthians 9:12; Galatians 5:13; Ephesians 4:11–13; Colossians 3:23–24; 1 Timothy 6:2; Revelation 2:19.

To complete the book of Hebrews during this twelve-part study, read Hebrews 13:1–25.

JOURNALING

What humble act of service can I offer to God today?